Illinois Deserves Better:
The Ironclad Case FOR an Illinois Constitutional Convention

John C. A. Bambenek &
Bruno Behrend

Copyright © John C. A. Bambenek & Bruno Behrend

All rights reserved. No part of this publication may be reproduced or transmitted in any form or by any means, electronic or mechanical, including photocopy, or any information storage and retrieval system now known or to be invented, without permission in writing from the authors, except by a reviewer who wished to quote brief passages in connection with a review written for inclusion in a magazine, newspaper, publication or broadcast.

Bambenek, John C. A. & Behrend, Bruno

Illinois Deserves Better: The Ironclad Case for an Illinois Constitutional Convention / Bambenek, John C. A. & Behrend, Bruno – Charleston, SC : BookSurge Publishing, © 2008.

ISBN-13: 9781419696732

ISBN-10: 1-4196-9673-4

Published by BookSurge Publishing

For more information contact:

Illinois Citizens Coalition

www.illinoiscitizenscoalition.com

Contents

Introduction 4
The State of the State 8
The Constitutional Convention Process 20
Arguments against a Convention 27
Potential Reforms 35

Introduction

On November 4th, 2008, Illinois citizens will have a once in a generation opportunity to call a Constitutional Convention. If you stop reading this book after this paragraph, please take away this singularly important message. **If a better Illinois and more honest government is your goal, then there is no intellectually sound reason to vote "No" on this ballot question.** This book will prove that proposition.

The state of Illinois is facing a financial crisis, which, if not addressed, will lead this state into bankruptcy. The state is also facing a political crisis with yet another governor under federal investigation, elected offices being passed down like feudal titles and a General Assembly that is simply unresponsive to the needs of the citizenry.

Important questions can be asked about our state. For instance, how is it that one of the largest states in the Union ranks 48th in its economic outlook? How did we get stuck with a widely unpopular governor who has become renowned in his ineffectiveness? How does a state with a balanced budget requirement in its constitution amass a $106 billion debt? Most importantly, what can we as average citizens do to turn the tide of broken government?

The current constitution of Illinois requires that every 20 years a referendum be placed on the ballot asking the voters if they wish to have a constitutional convention to rewrite the constitution and/or propose amendments to the current constitution. The convention then must submit any desired changes to the voters to be ratified with later referenda questions. This represents the *only* opportunity for citizens to directly impact the sorry state of affairs in Illinois.

It is important to note that a constitution is not a document with which to enshrine special interests, niche issues or to entirely supplant the legislative or executive functions of government. A constitution should accomplish two things: provide for a sound framework of governance and to establish and protect fundamental rights. It is with this understanding that we approach the question of a convention.

Many of the problems in Illinois can be traced to the election of politicians who are somewhat less than honorable. A great many problems, to be sure, would be solved by simply having better governors, legislators and local elected officials. However, a constitution is designed to limit the amount of damage a bad office-holder can do. It is written with an understanding that sometimes those who seek political power are doing so with impure intentions. An example may help illustrate the point.

The federal constitution, as does the constitutions of every state in this country, provides for a three-branch form of government with a system of checks and balances. This system was devised so that self-interested legislators would balance the power of a self-interested executive who would also be balanced by self-interested members of the judiciary. The constitution was written with an inherent distrust of elected officials. It didn't make sense to the founding fathers or the authors of any of the state constitutions to place their foundation of freedom on the hopes of simply electing honest politicians.

Likewise, the case of Illinois' constitution cannot be simply resolved with anecdotes that we need to simply elect better leaders. There are structural problems in the current constitution itself that are used by power-brokers and vested interests to keep a corrupt system from being effectively challenged by the voters. Legislative districting, or more accurately gerrymandering, allows legislatures and political parties to draw their own boundaries with the overt purpose of keeping as many seats for the General Assembly as uncompetitive as possible. This insulates these legislators from the will of the people because they do not have to worry about reelection. Voters should pick their leaders; leaders should not be able to pick their voters.

A constitution cannot nor should not try to reverse the results of an election. It should, however, create a framework of governance that allows the greatest possible amount of public participation and keep the bar of entry of those wishing to run for office as low as possible. Right now many good and talented citizens are kept out of public office by a system that is designed to keep insiders, and only insiders, with a firm grip on the reigns of power.

The particular reforms that are pursued in a convention should be those high-level items that fit into the purpose of a constitution. Ethics legislation, as good and necessary as it is, should not be established in a constitution. However, legislative redistricting is a process that is currently in the constitution and it should be reformed there. The balanced budget requirement is currently in the constitution and it needs to be reformed so that the legislature cannot count "debt" as "income" to balance the budget. Fundamental rights such as open ballot access, open primaries, citizen-initiated referenda and eminent domain reform should also be addressed in a constitution.

A quick glance at the biographies of the authors of this book will show that we are both conservatives and it may be tempting to simply write this effort off as a conservative attempt at a takeover of the state. However, many of these reforms were developed with many others of wildly varying political persuasions. As we have gone across the state to talk about the convention and these reforms, we have seen that honest conservatives, libertarians, progressives, greens and independents all have remarkably similar views on these constitutional reforms. In fact, many of the groups that advocate against a convention *do not* disagree with many of the reforms we are pushing. A constitution must create a framework for good governance that serves all the people.

The biggest driving factor of those who push for citizens to vote no on a convention is fear. Fear that a "runaway convention" would make the state worse and fear that no reforms could get through a convention because the vested interests will stop it. We have become so dejected in this state we are afraid to even try to fix the system.

The facts are that the state is going broke and it is dramatically corrupt. Preemptive surrender will only accomplish getting more of the same. If we do nothing, the state *will* go bankrupt because those in power simply have no plan with which to fix the problem. Education funding reform is the top priority of

Illinois voters going into this year's election and no movement on that issue has occurred in the General Assembly for *40 years!* Voting "yes" on a constitutional convention will give the voters the opportunity for change. The best one could hope for by voting "no" is getting the status quo.

Our political system is paralyzed with back-biting and corruption and has become unable and/or unwilling to act on desperately needed issues. A constitutional convention is our last hope to be able to enact the necessary governmental reforms to end the deadlock and cycle of corruption. Doing nothing will ensure we get a state that is bankrupt, that shirks its' pension obligations, the lays even more onerous tax burdens on businesses and hardworking families while continuing the "pay-to-play" politics that has earned this state federal investigation after federal investigation.

The situation is dire, to be sure, and we plan to lay out exactly how this bad situation is a product, in part, of deficiencies in the current constitution. We will lay out the referendum and convention process to show how a convention can occur that will not only be protected against "runaway" ideas that make the state worse, but can produce badly needed reforms. Lastly, we'll lay out our platform for a new constitution in detail to show how we plan to fix the problems.

There is only one thing this plan needs to work: hope. If the citizens of Illinois do not believe that we can get a better government, we won't. We must believe that Illinois deserves better. But more than just hope is needed, effort is required too. Honest people regardless of political affiliation need to stand up and demand better.

Getting a convention will not happen automatically and certainly, without taking the time, effort, and money needed, reform-minded delegates will not be elected. We must believe that Illinois deserves better and then act on it. Now is a time for bold action to design a constitution we can be proud of. Our General Assembly and elected leaders have failed, it falls to us now to take up the call and address the problems our state faces.

The State of the State

The State of Illinois is Broke

Does that Chapter title scare you? Is it a tad hyperbolic? Don't take our word for it. Read the Civic Committee Report of the Commercial Club of Chicago.

> "Illinois is headed toward financial implosion. The State's liabilities and unfunded commitments exceed its assets by over $106 billion. The State has failed to set aside the amounts necessary to pay employee/retiree pensions and health benefits and to pay amounts currently owed to health care providers under Medicaid. The State has also failed to fund K-12 education at the "foundation level." These liabilities and unfunded commitments are growing rapidly. Yet, the State continues to spend or commit to spend billions more than it takes in each year."[1]

If that isn't convincing, let's look at this report from the *Institute for Truth in Accounting*. As an example, even though the budget was "balanced" in 2004, the state's audited financial report indicated the state had a deficit of $2.5 billion.

"The state's constitution requires a balanced budget, so how can the politicians claim the budget is balanced when it is not? (See box)

> Article VIII Section 2(b) states:
>
> *The General Assembly by law shall make appropriations for all expenditures of public funds by the State. Appropriations for a fiscal year shall not exceed funds estimated by the General Assembly to be available during that year.*

The answer is that it all depends on how you count. The politicians do not calculate the budget on a cash basis or an accrual basis; the two most generally recognized bases of accounting. The state of Illinois is using the same accounting

---

[1] Facing Facts – A Report on the Civic Committee's Task Force for State Finance, Civic Committee of the Commercial Club of Chicago. 2006, Page 1.

gimmicks that led to the downfall of huge American corporations."[2]

For decades Illinois' elected officials have claimed the state budget has been balanced. As mentioned above, the Constitution even requires a "balanced budget."

What we have in the Constitution certainly looks like a balanced budget clause, but the dirty little secret is that the **state budget has not been balanced** pretty much since the 1970s. Once the legislators and the Executive branch realized that debt could be morphed into "revenues," they have been rolling over increasingly large deficits for decades. As we've noted above, this is why the state has $106 billion in unfunded liabilities. *This alone is reason enough to revisit the Constitution.*

The fiscal year budget is only a current snap shot of Illinois' financial condition. The whole movie is going to get much worse. Last year, the legislature and the governor engaged in a never-ending session to provide transit funding "bailout for the CTA/RTA/Pace system. If you rode Chicago's CTA in the winter of 2007, advertising space on the trains was replaced by appeals to support new taxes and avoid a "doomsday scenario" of cuts in bus routes and increases in fares. The fight in Springfield was over which Illinois citizens are going to be taxed to bailout another Chicago/Cook County boondoggle.

Another item on the agenda in early 2008 is a "Capital Program" for Illinois. The Governor wants a "Capital Program" for roads, schools and public transit (separate from the current CTA "bailout" debate). Of course, capital programs, which rely on the sales of billions in government bonds, need stable revenue streams, so the debate is which revenue stream to tap for the "capital-spending plan."

The options on the table are a tax increase, some other tax increases, and expanding gambling, which will eventually lead to more tax increases. If that isn't enough, there is always auctioning

---

[2] Illinois Grande Illusion – A Guide to Bringing Truth to the Illinois Budget, Institute for Truth in Accounting, 2006, Page 3.

off the toll roads and the lottery. It worked with the "sale" of the Thompson center.

If things appear bad across the state, they are arguably worse in Cook County. Again, as we write these pages, Todd Stroger, the Cook County Board President who inherited his position because of his ailing father, is angling for aggressive sales tax increases for Cook County residents. If he didn't get these tax increases, he threatened to institute a four dollar "line tax" on every phone line and cell phone number sourced out of Cook County

Not 2 months after the passage of a sales tax increase giving Cook County the highest sales tax in the nation, Stroger immediately called for even more tax increases while the news media reported on the large raises given to his relative in Cook County government.

As citizens of Chicago and Cook County fret over their soon to be increased taxes, the rest of Illinois citizens are sure to be angered over yet another tax increase. Downstate and western Illinois voters fear that they will once again see their state representatives and senators vote for tax dollars flowing into Chicago and Cook County in exchange for a few table scraps of pork. Former Speaker of the House Dennis Hastert has retired from Congress to take advantage of lobbying opportunities. Who is his first big client? The interests lobbying for a "capital bill" we mentioned.

One important question that gets lost in the debate over CTA bailouts and capital spending programs, and State and County tax increases is, "What happened to all the money that has flowed into government coffers in the past few years?"

The Illinois State budget has grown from $23 billion in FY 2003 (Governor Blagojevich's first budget) to $28.8 billion in FY 2007. This represents a 25% increase over 4 years, or about 6.25% per year.[3] Where did all that money go?

---

[3] This number is for the General Revenue Fund only. When you add Federal funds for block grants and other programs, the Illinois state budget for 2007 is about $59 billion dollars.

There are so many answers. The growth in Medicaid is part of the problem. Another area of rapid (and accelerating) growth is the payout for government pensions. Across the state, teachers and administrators are retiring, taking advantage of retirement benefits. The funding of such benefits is supposed to be covered by the respective retirement systems. The problem is that each of these retirement systems is dramatically under-funded, or, if not under-funded, then getting yearly cash infusions from the state's General Fund.

While the General Fund is paying off one pension fund to keep it solvent, it is failing to pay into other pension funds so the state can meet its other obligations. In 2006, the entire budget was "balanced" simply by the General Assembly and the Governor deciding not to pay into the Teachers Retirement System. In fact, the state has never met its pension obligations since the ratification of the 1970 Constitution.

Here is an even more frightening answer to the question "Where did the money go?" No one knows. In a November, 2007 article in the Springfield Journal-Register, the writer reports that,

> "Auditor General William Holland reported Wednesday that he had tried to research whether some government services could be consolidated but found there was no master list of programs.

His office then surveyed state agencies and found about 1,750 programs. But Holland said there are probably even more out there, because some agencies did not give him a detailed list.[4]

We could go on for hours detailing the games played by Illinois' political class. Stem Cell research was voted down, but $10 million of funding reappeared out of one Illinois many "slush funds." Regardless of where you stand on the stem cell research issue, it should give any honest citizen pause that a governor can overrule the legislature by fiat and establish and fund a program specifically rejected by the General Assembly.

As we type these pages, the news of the day is how Governor Blagojevich "gave" $1,000,000 to a church that burned

---

[4] Much of what state does remains a mystery to auditor, Christopher Wills, Associated Press for the Springfield Journal Register, November 01, 2007

down. The money actually went to a now defunct daycare center in that church, and the money is either spent, or locked up in a lawsuit. The Church doesn't have the money, and the daycare center isn't caring for any kids.

Millions of dollars of pork are distributed at the discretion of legislators, but citizens never get see the process by which these decisions are made. Billions of dollars of school construction have taken place across the state, 250 projects completed by using legislative loopholes to circumvent voter referenda. Whether the examples run into the millions, or the billions, the Illinois taxpayer pays the price.

This is Illinois today- A virtual banana republic of legislative log rolling, back scratching, and "pay to play" public/private partnerships. This dangerously shaky house of cards is about to be hit by a financial storm of un-payable bills and falling revenues.

Yet, almost no politician in the state has the courage to demand budget and spending reforms that would open up the state to citizen review and fiscal sanity. Neither party, nor a single leader has emerged to challenge the culture of spending and waste that has become the hallmark of this once respected state. This leads us to ask, "What is wrong with Illinois' political class?"

Illinois' Political System is Broken

Anyone who reads the headlines coming out of Springfield over the summer of 2007 understands that there is something seriously wrong with Illinois politics. The Democratic Party, dominating at every level of government, is locked in an endless squabble over who gets the goodies in their patronage system. The Republican Party, disorganized and powerless, is reaping the whirlwind from their attempt to sow a patronage system of their own. Region by region and headline by headline, we see an increasingly *corrupt* government.

As you read through this book, you will be introduced to many portions of the Illinois Constitution that insulate "government" from citizen oversight. This has created an environment where politicians can obfuscate much of the process

> **Is "Corrupt" too strong a word?**
>
> Many people may object to our use of the word "corrupt" in describing something as broad as "Illinois' political class." We do not apologize. Corruption takes many forms, and most of them are not "indictable offences." As you find out more and more about Illinois government, you will see that it allows many people to engage in things that are "wrong" even if they are not illegal.
>
> We think "corrupt" is a valid term for these acts and actors.

and machinery of government, allowing them to direct jobs, contracts, benefits, to various industries and individuals.

Those news reports you see in the headlines, detailing possible wrongdoing are the 10% of the iceberg that can be seen. We hope to give you a glimpse of what goes on beneath the surface, and how the current Constitution has created and protected this state of affairs.

Who Runs Illinois?

On paper, Illinois is run by the vast numbers of elected officials and bureaucrats that work in state and local government. Your average voter would believe that there is a diffusion of power among these people and entities. In reality, 6 or 7 very powerful political actors run Illinois, and most Representatives and Municipal officials are merely bit players.

Illinois is run by a group that politicians that pundits call **"the four tops**." If the 2 major parties are equally balanced, or one party might threaten to take over one chamber of the legislature in the next election, then these four tops are the House and Senate Majority and Minority leaders. Their job is to get together with the Governor and bang out an agreement over who gets what money, what programs get expanded, renamed, or restructured. The four tops tell their "caucus" (your State Reps. or Senators) how to vote.

In today's political configuration - with a powerless Republican Party, and Democrat party in control of every branch of Illinois government - the state is **not** run by the Governor and the "4 tops." Today, Illinois is run by what we call "**3 men in a room**." This would be the House Speaker, the President of the Senate, and the Governor.

Of course, if the 3 men in a room can't get together to decide all the important issues on the state budget, then the minority party may regain some power, as the Constitution mandates that if a budget isn't passed by June 1st, then a $3/5^{th}$ majority is required to pass a budget. 2007 was a banner year for the 3 men in a room. Their personality conflicts created a series of 30-day budget extensions, with the final agreement on the budget months late (and few million dollars short).

A service organization for non-profits called the "Donor's Forum" has an unintentionally humorous "Road Map" poster detailing the budget process of the Illinois Government.[5] If you thought our description of the process of dividing up the budget was too cynical, just read their poster, a portion of which is reproduced on the next page.

---

[5] Some one should write a book about governments funding not-for-profits and the mischief that may cause, but we lack the time to cover that here.

http://www.donorsforum.org/forms_pdf/ILBudget_poster.pdf

BUDGET INTRODUCED
FEBRUARY

By law, the Governor must present his budget to a joint session of the General Assembly no later than the third Wednesday in February of each year. Copies are available online at: www.state.il.us/budget

"The Governor shall prepare and submit to the General Assembly, at a time prescribed by law, a State budget for the ensuing fiscal year… Proposed expenditures shall not exceed funds estimated to be available for the fiscal year as shown in the budget."
— Illinois Constitution: Article 9 Section 2

BUDGET HEARING
MARCH – APRIL

Legislative review of the Governor's budget begins in March and April before the House and Senate appropriation committees. Committees may adopt amendments to change the funding levels recommended by the Governor. Each amendment to the budget must be accompanied by a fiscal note, which describes its fiscal implications.

- A good way for nonprofits to influence the budget process is to submit support for their issues in advance to Committee staff, attend Appropriation Committee hearings, and testify on the importance of a funding level, program, or policy.

FINAL NEGOTIATIONS AND VOTE MAY

The Governor, the four party leaders, and budget negotiators meet to work out the final budget. These meetings are closed to the public. Thus, in order to influence the process, it is critical that nonprofits work closely with their supporters in the General Assembly to influence these negotiations.

The Illinois Constitution requires a 3/5 vote of legislators to approve the budget after June 1 but a simple majority before that date.

Closed to the public?

Did you ever vote for this process? Do you know anyone who did?

And here you thought your State Representative or Senator had a voice in the process. Few people in Illinois realize that their elected legislators are there more for the purposes of creating the appearance of representation. As you can see from the *Donor's Forum* poster, they pretty much do what the leadership tells them.

You also need to know that if your State Representative or Senator bucks their party leader on an important vote (decided by 3 men in a room), they are likely to receive a well-funded challenger in the next primary. If you are one of those citizens that have been getting a queasy feeling that you don't really have any representation in Springfield, now you know why.

Certainly, some legislators have more power than others, as they may provide more electoral clout or fundraising acumen than others. Of course, if they happen to represent a district in Cook County or Chicago, they have an even greater chance of attaining a level of clout, as the Illinois Constitution gives Cook County the lion's share of political power.

While this rankles many people outside the Chicago Metropolitan area, it should rankle the citizens inside even more. They have the appearance of electoral clout, given their numbers and treatment in the Constitution, but it is the political class that is empowered, not the citizen of Chicago or Cook County. The next time your Cook County Board member reminds you that Cook County has 'Home Rule,' remind them that this only means they have more power to tax and regulate absent any citizen oversight.

Regardless, aside from the 4 tops and/or 3 men in a room, the Mayor of Chicago and the President of the Cook County Board, have enormous power in the state, simply by operation of "machine" politics.

In theory, the state is supposed to be a separate entity capable of separate power structures than Chicago and Cook County. In practice, the clout of the Chicago and Cook County apparatus, combined with the large numbers of voters there, provides a one-two punch in the gut of Illinois taxpayers. The money and organization provided by the heavily populated city and collar counties allow Cook County bosses to wield immense power. So when you see those news reports, with all talk about personalities and parties, and the distracting rhetoric of Democrat versus Republican and left versus right, remember that much of it is a sideshow.

On the surface, this exercise is all about the "hard choices" and "tough stances" that our leaders work on to do "the peoples' business." Beneath the surface, jobs, contracts, patronage, and pork are doled out according to which political group and what industries have the most access to Legislative and Executive leadership. They aren't doing the people's business.

The financial and political situation in Illinois has given us an electorate that is increasingly disillusioned, disengaged or just plain angry. Some people have just packed up and gone to other states. They know things are bad, but they won't believe that any re-engagement in the process will provide any benefit. The political advantages built into the existing system, combined with the disengaged electorate has now created a situation where there is no real chance of improvement under the current political system.

Ask yourself under what scenario Illinois will turn some financial or political corner. Is any politician telling you that we must cut spending, or possibly freeze it for a few years, so as to use the natural revenue growth to fund pension shortfalls?

Have any politicians talked about the pension and benefit abuses of the state and municipal governments, or the number of political positions and contracts to their friends? Perhaps one or two have mentioned it, but no one has proposed scaling back on the rate of growth of government or the trimming of benefits.

Though most know that a financial debacle is looming, Illinois' politicians are clamoring for any "revenue enhancement" they can find to fund the gaps they have created. They are making spending promises they know they can't keep in the hope of getting tax increases. These new revenues won't fund the promises. They are needed to fund pension obligations.

Illinois citizens need to understand the scope of the problem. We are sailing into rough seas with incompetent leaders.

Are Republicans the Answer?

There used to be a party that stood for fiscal discipline and lower taxation. You may have heard of them. They were called Republicans. There are some people in Illinois Government who call themselves Republicans, but you won't hear them talk about fiscal responsibility or returning control of Illinois' government to its citizens. If they did, they might start winning elections again, but they appear too timid (or connected) to try.

What about returning Republicans to power? Will the Republican Party improve the situation in Illinois? Why would they? They were abusing governmental power as well.

They excoriate the Democrats for merely doing more of what they did with 25 years of executive power. Much of their posturing is merely an attempt to return to power for the chance of exercising it. Their only "platform" is pointing out the personality conflicts and incompetence of the Democrats - who are merely doing what Republicans have done for years - only more brazenly.

Is there any hope?

We would like to be optimistic about Illinois' prospects, but there isn't anything on the political horizon to be optimistic about, save one thing.

As bad things are, there is one piece of good news. Despite the fact that Illinois has one of the most ambiguous and poorly written constitutions in the United States, it contains one article (and even that is ambiguous) that allows Illinois citizens the opportunity to take their state back from the entranced interests that are literally eating the state alive.

The Illinois Constitution gives the citizens the opportunity to vote on a Constitutional Convention every 20 years. That vote is coming on the same day of the November Presidential election of 2008. This means that on November 4th, 2008, the citizens of Illinois can rise up and begin the process of taking their state back from the entrenched and incompetent political class.

This clause was put into the Constitution of 1970 specifically to give the citizens the opportunity to act when the Legislature was unable or unwilling to do so. We are at that point now. Concerned citizens of all political parties and stripes should do everything in their power to make sure that people vote "Yes" to a Constitutional Convention.

The state of Illinois is broke, and its politics are broken. Whether the issue is a recall of the Governor, a ballot initiative to impose term limits, allowing citizens the right to a referendum to rollback their property taxes, or adding provisions that open all levels of Illinois to citizen oversight, there is no scenario whereby any of these things can come to pass – **except for a Constitutional Convention.**

The rest of this book discusses some of the things that will improve Illinois Government, along with process by which the citizens can make a Constitutional Convention a success.

We will also address arguments against a Constitutional Convention. Some of these arguments – that it might cost the state $80 to 100 million dollars, for example - are silly on their face. Other arguments – that it might be possible to get a Constitution that may be worse than what we have, for example – are deserving of a reasoned response. We intend to address some of arguments these issues in this book, as well as during the 2008 campaign to get a "yes" vote.

The Constitutional Convention Process

The following text is directly from Article 14 of the Illinois Constitution.

Article XIV

SECTION 1. CONSTITUTIONAL CONVENTION

a) Whenever three-fifths of the members elected to each house of the General Assembly so direct, the question of whether a Constitutional Convention should be called shall be submitted to the electors at the general election next occurring at least six months after such legislative direction.

b) If the question of whether a Convention should be called is not submitted during any twenty-year period, the Secretary of State shall submit such question at the general election in the twentieth year following the last submission.

c) The vote on whether to call a Convention shall be on a separate ballot. A Convention shall be called if approved by three-fifths of those voting on the question or a majority of those voting in the election.

d) The General Assembly, at the session following approval by the electors, by law shall provide for the Convention and for the election of two delegates from each Legislative District; designate the time and place of the Convention's first meeting which shall be within three months after the election of delegates; fix and provide for the pay of delegates and officers; and provide for expenses necessarily incurred by the Convention.

e) To be eligible to be a delegate a person must meet the same eligibility requirements as a member of the General Assembly. Vacancies shall be filled as provided by law.

f) The Convention shall prepare such revision of or amendments to the Constitution as it deems necessary. Any proposed revision or amendments approved by a majority of the delegates elected shall be submitted to the electors in such manner as the Convention determines, at an election designated or called by the Convention occurring not less than two nor more than six months after the Convention's adjournment. Any revision or amendments proposed by the Convention shall be published with explanations, as the Convention provides, at least one month preceding the election.

g) The vote on the proposed revision or amendments shall be on a separate ballot. Any proposed revision or amendments shall become effective, as the Convention provides, if approved by a majority of those voting on the question.

Defining the Convention Process

If you've read through the text of Article 14, you notice that the Constitutional Convention process encompasses three separate elections. The first part of that process is the November 2008 vote. The second is the election of delegates, and the third is the ratification of amendments or a new constitution by the people of Illinois. This short description leaves out the entire process of what actually goes on in the convention. In the next few pages, we will provide more detail for each part of the process.

The Convention Referendum

According to Article 14 of the Illinois Constitution, the question of a Constitutional convention comes up automatically in 2008. For a convention to be called, it must pass by 60% (3/5 majority) of the vote. If the question falls short of 60%, the citizens of the Illinois must either wait another 20 years for the question to arise again, or they can hold their breath and wait for 3/5 of the General Assembly to reform Illinois.

The politics of the convention vote are usually easy to predict. Early in the process (where we are in February of 2008), the idea of a convention usually has majority support. As more and more people start to discuss it, interest and support rises slightly. By the time late summer rolls around, the entrenched interests on both the left and right (unions, utilities, and state contractors) start the process of attacking the idea of a constitutional convention.

These opponents will usually bring up standard arguments like "Don't fix what isn't broken." In the current environment in Illinois, the electorate will see "don't fix what isn't broken" as downright silly. Therefore, we will probably be subjected to an argument that is almost as silly. We will be told "the people who run Illinois are so bad, that if we have a convention, they will make things even worse." We will address that argument later.

If you are reading this book because you have an interested in improving the State of Illinois, you should keep one important factor in mind. Voting "yes" on a Constitutional convention offers the opportunity for reform. Voting "no" offers no opportunity at all. It is a vote for the status quo *at best*.

Electing Delegates

Should the question pass, Article 14 then directs the Illinois legislature to set out the process for the election of delegates and the time and place for a convention. This brings us to the second -- and probably the most important -- election. Article 14 calls for the election of two delegates from each" Legislative (Senate) District."

This means that 118 delegates will have the opportunity to amend, or completely rewrite the Illinois Constitution. We think this represents a wonderful opportunity for concerned citizens to reenter the political arena in Illinois. As we have traveled across the State of Illinois, presenting our ideas on the opportunity created by a convention, we have noticed that many decent people seem interested in either helping a secure yes vote or to run as a delegate themselves.

We believe this experience represents one of the most powerful arguments against the timid souls who believe that the existing political class will maintain control of the delegate election process. We don't think they can.

Imagine a delegate race between a professional, dedicated and articulate citizen, and a party operative from one of the two dominant parties. Let us assume that the dedicated citizen is running on a set of principles and ideas they believe in while the "experienced" party hack is running on "their record." Even in Illinois jaundiced political climate, we think the citizen delegate stands a very good chance. This is not to say that the existing political class doesn't have a few cards up their sleeves.

Additionally, there are no incumbents in the race for a convention delegate. Any political consultant will tell you it is *far* easier to run for an open seat than against someone already in office. Further, full-time office holders would likely have to resign their office to serve as a short-term constitutional convention delegate, perhaps relinquishing their office permanently. Lastly, legislators are specifically prohibited from drawing two salaries at the same time, so unless they could manage to ensure the General

Assembly would finish their session on time (or early) and that a convention would be finished before the session began again, they could not serve either. The 1969-1970 convention only had two sitting legislators serve as delegates and that was before the "double-dipping" prohibition and back when the General Assembly was not marred in partisan bickering that gridlocked their work. In a nutshell, most "established names" in Illinois politics would not or could not run for delegate seats.

Astute readers of the text of Article 14 may note that the Legislature is empowered to "provide for the ...election of the delegates." This begs the question as to just how much power the legislature has to define the convention. Based upon the text, they could call an election of delegates almost immediately. This might empower the two dominant parties (and their patrons), in that they would have the jump on organization and candidate selection. On the other hand, they might decide to schedule the election for delegates as far out as November of 2010. Under that scenario, the existing parties would be able to take advantage of voter turnout, while also allowing more time for vetting delegate candidates.

There is also the question of whether the election of delegates would be "non-partisan" – meaning that there would be no party identification on the delegate ballots.

In the 1970 Constitution convention, the state held an open primary followed by an open general election. In this process, there may have been numerous candidates on the primary ballot. After the primary, the top four vote-getters ran for the two delegates seats. The fact is that at this point in time, there is no predicting what the legislature will do.

However, the most likely scenario is that the delegates will be chosen in an open (non-partisan) election, similar to the way that Illinois residents fill seats for local trustees and school boards. Citizens who meet the criteria (age and residency of 2 years) set forth for Legislators; will be required to collect a certain amount of signatures (another area where the legislators can "rig" the selection by favoring existing party apparatus). If this is the case, delegates will be selected in a nonpartisan election (open and without party identification).

After consulting with experts and after reviewing what happened in 1969 and 70, we have determined that the loose language of Article 14 allows the Legislature a great deal of latitude in deciding upon the time and manner of the election. The existing political establishment of Illinois therefore, has the ability to control the process up to the election of delegates (and therefore play some of their usual games). However, we think that there is still a high probability that a good deal of "new blood" will make it into the convention.

We base this belief upon the experience of the last convention, where many concerned citizens with no previous political experience took part in the process. To be sure, some of these people - Mike Madigan and Dawn Clark-Netsch - are now familiar names in Illinois. Furthermore, the former mayor of Chicago, Richard J. Daley, made sure that his son, Richard M. Daley, won his delegate race. The existing political class of Illinois is certain to get a number of delegates elected. This is no reason to believe that the more enlightened citizens of Illinois won't succeed in seating many new delegates. The failed policies of the existing political class almost guarantee this.

The Convention

It is easy to define the general process of what goes on in a convention. It is far more difficult to define what might come out of that process.

As Article 14 states, the General Assembly (this means those elected in November of 2008) will;

> "Designate the time and place of the Convention's first meeting which shall be within three months after the election of delegates; fix and provide for the pay of delegates and officers; and provide for expenses necessarily incurred by the Convention."

The General Assembly provides a framework, but it is the delegates elected to the convention will decide what happens at the convention. Nothing in Article 14 allows the legislature to dictate the outcome or even the process.

Therefore, once the convention is seated, it is the delegates who will decide on whether to have committees, who will sit on those committees, and how the leadership is decided. Furthermore, the delegates will be able to decide whether they wish to add, subtract, or change some of the articles of the existing Constitution, or whether they wish to rewrite the entire document.

Readers should also be aware of the possibility that the convention might not result in any changes at all. While seemingly unlikely, Article 14 does require that any changes made by the delegates pass out of the convention by majority vote. If there is no majority vote for any changes, then no changes can be sent to the voters for ratification.

That said, should there be a convention, it is almost certain that it will result in changes being presented to the voters.

Ratification

As Article 14 provides, the citizens of Illinois will get an opportunity to ratify (or turn down) any changes made to the Constitution by the convention delegates. This ratification must take place no sooner than two months and no later than six months after the close of the convention.

The ratification vote presents one of the strongest arguments against those who fear a "runaway convention." As bad as the political leadership is Illinois, (and the citizenry bears some of the blame for this state of affairs) we still trust the citizens to properly decide whether to ratify any changes.

Once presented with clear and concise language on specific changes to their Constitution, Illinois citizens, along with the interests that wish to promote and/or defeat any changes, will engage in the necessary debate that is currently lacking among our current political class. This dynamic (of empowering citizens) also presents strong evidence that there will be no radical swings to the left or right.

Whatever one thinks of the current political climate, there is very little evidence that either of the social-issue extremes in Illinois has the power to enact their agenda through a convention. We believe the citizens of Illinois will have the common sense to reject any extreme constitutional changes. They will however, ratify a more open, and honest government that puts them back in control.

In fact, if you review the entire constitution convention process, from the November 2008 referendum through to the ratification, you can see that it presents the citizens of Illinois a once-in-a-generation opportunity to reengage themselves in Illinois policymaking. We believe this will radically change the political dynamic that currently exists. We think this change effectively addresses the few reasonable arguments against a "yes" vote.

Arguments against a Convention

As mentioned before, there are some silly arguments against a constitutional convention, and a few that merit a discussion. Let's get one of the silliest out of the way right off the bat.

The convention will "cost money"

At recent panel discussion on the convention (aired on the Illinois Channel), Lt. Gov. Pat Quinn and Rep. John Fritchey argued the "pro-convention" side, while Dawn Clark-Netsch (former Comptroller) and Nancy Kazak (a former State Rep.) argued against a convention. At one point, Ms. Kazak opined that the convention would "cost too much money."

This is a ridiculous argument. Here we are, in a state approaching a financial crisis brought about by a flawed constitution and an irresponsible and un-serious political class, and we are being told that we shouldn't spend $30-80 million on a convention that might fix the problem?! We should consider $100 million a small price to pay! At the same time, the Illinois Senate is trying to raid over $50 million for frivolous pork barrel projects. The money is there. In reality, according to an estimate by the General Assembly, it would only cost $9-10 million. It should be important to note, the General Assembly sets the budget for a convention, so their estimate will basically be the entirety of what is appropriated.

We have a **$106 BILLION** problem, and we can't fund the process that will put 118 citizens in a room to fix it? $6 to $8 **billion** is the interest payment on our debt obligations. Our innate politeness won't allow us to treat this argument in the manner it deserves. It suffices to call it ridiculous.

The "Illinois political class" will control the Convention

As harsh critics of the "Illinois' Political Class," we should seriously consider this critique of a constitutional convention. The argument is as follows.

> *"Given the quality of political leadership in Illinois, along with the jaundiced electorate that put them there, a convention will yield the same poor leadership. Therefore, a convention is a bad idea."*

At first glance, this argument seems reasonable. After all, who will step forward to run for delegate? Who indeed?

First off, we find it somewhat humorous that the people making this argument are members of the "political class" themselves.

"I wouldn't want to join a club that would have me"

Well, Mr. or Mrs. Illinois Political Class, we can only say that we are in full agreement. The good news, (for convention supporters) is that the electorate of Illinois will likely agree. We found this precious little tidbit on a western suburban community forum. The person was describing a speaking engagement attended by Senator Dan Cronin.

> I once heard Dan Cronin complaining about the current administration and the majority party. ...I asked him if he might be implicitly suggesting that a *constitutional convention* be a desirable goal. He said no, because it would only make the system worse. I pressed him...He still was against the idea. He said the same people now in the legislature would become delegates to the convention; what good would that be?[6]

While we agree that packing the convention with members of Illinois' existing political class would be less than we would hope for, we don't think that is how things would work out.

Will Mayor Daley and Mike Madigan get some of their people in there? Yes. Will the downstate Republicans elect some delegates of their own? Sure. The fact is that, while some of these folks will be seated at the convention; two factors radically change the dynamics of delegate races.

First, the existing financial and political situation in Illinois will is dramatically different than in 1970. The state is in far worse shape, and the voters know it. Should we be successful in getting a "yes" vote, the idea that the electorate will place "the same people"

---

[6]http://glen-llyn.com/eve/forums/a/tpc/f/190106284/m/8581050884/p/3

in the convention is very unlikely. Voters are not stupid and it is telling that our elected leaders keep telling us that the voters cannot be trusted.

Certainly, members of the political class may have some advantages regarding political machinery and name recognition. On the other hand, imagine yourself (a dedicated and concerned Illinois citizen willing to run for a delegate seat) in a debate with a State Representative or one of their lackeys. Democrat or Republican, it really doesn't matter – you point to them, and you point to the condition of the state - and ask the voter, "Are you really going to elect the people who put us in this position as a delegate to the convention?"

The answer in very many cases will be "no." Decent and dedicated citizens will be seated at the convention. We don't even need a majority. All we need is a voting block of decent people. As much as the Illinois Political Class has done to force decent citizens out of the political process, we believe there are still few million left who are up to the task of fixing Illinois. The radically different dynamics of a convention is the perfect vehicle to put them in that position.

Second, there is always the chance that a member of Illinois political class, as bad as they might be, may just turn out to be a good delegate. There is some thing qualitatively different about writing a constitution and skewing legislation to favor the interest groups that fund your campaigns.

Lastly, and most importantly, because of the length of a convention, most sitting politicians will not be able to be part of the convention. A legislator could not be a delegate at the same time because the time frames would overlap and the law and precedent are clear that a politician can't be paid for two jobs at the same time. A legislator would have to resign their seat in the General Assembly and risk losing it forever simply to hold a part-time job as a delegate. In the 1968 convention, only 2 sitting legislators were delegates as well and that only happened because the term of the general assembly was much more manageable than it is today. In short, all full-time politicians will likely not be able to run for delegates without sacrificing their elected offices.

The voters would have to support a convention in large numbers for this to happen. After coming out with such large support, it is simply illogical to believe the voters will simply tune out after voting for such an important event. It will take, however, good honest people of all political stripes to run for delegate and push a reform agenda. It is also naïve to think that voting yes for a convention means all work is completed on reform as well.

It's the Illinois Leadership, not the Constitution

This argument against a convention is the flip side of the last one – that the political class will win the delegate races. In another panel discussion featuring Dawn Clark Netsch, she commented that;

> "We don't have a constitutional crisis in the state of Illinois. We have a leadership crisis," [Netsch] said, adding: "There are no constitutional barriers to resolving the issues that have been plaguing us for the last couple of years. The only thing that is missing is the kind of leadership that brings those issues finally to bear."

This view is echoed by connected interests on both sides of the political spectrum. The Illinois Business Round Table (IBRT) has a fancy booklet defending the existing Constitution. In it, they write,

> Despite concern with the current functional capability of state government, many of today's issues are neither the cause for nor remedied by constitutional change. **Illinois current constitutional framework is adequate, open, and not hostile to resolving the serious issues that confront the state today**.[7]

It is our position that both the IBRT and Netsch are wrong. **The "leadership crisis" is *a direct result* of Illinois' Constitution**. We won't get better leaders until we get constitution that allows them to get elected.

We've already showed how 5 or 3 men in a room divvy up the state budget. We've also discussed how legislative leaders can punish independent representatives by withholding funding or funding a challenger. This has lead to an insulated and inbred

---

[7] http://www.icjl.org/IBRTCon-Con.pdf

political class that will never encounter serious opposition as long as they don't buck the system.

The gerrymandering in Illinois is another reason why we citizens can't look forward to better leadership. We live in a state where politicians pick their voters instead of the other way around.

If we wanted to, we could write a whole book on the hundreds of ways the Illinois Constitution operates to destroy leadership. This book could discuss the overemphasis given to Cook County and the Chicago Metropolitan area.

It could talk about how the citizens have no recourse through ballot initiative or recall. We could do a chapter or two on how the lack of transparency destroys citizen oversight. We frankly don't have the time for such a book. Simply read the headlines across the state, and they make our case for us.

Over at Rich Miller's Capitol Fax website (an influential Illinois blog), one commentator attempted to make Netsch's point. He asked, *"What if we had a good Governor instead of this guy?"*

A good governor? Let's see...

Otto Kerner brought on the last convention, out of concerns over corruption and fiscal problems. **Richard Ogilvie** gave us the income tax. **Dan Walker** went to jail. **Jim Edgar** left amid questions about a contract with a company called MSI, and **George Ryan** is in jail. Our current governor, **Rod Blagojevich**, is a likely candidate for indictment and possibly jail.

Interestingly, **Jim Thompson** now seems to have a lucrative business defending Illinois governors. This is ironic, given that putting Otto Kerner behind bars launched his career.

On the legislative front, powerful entrenched leaders make sure that no one rises to a position where anyone can challenge the status quo. Leaders can unilaterally prevent good bills from coming to a vote, as they dole out Illinois' version of earmarks to the special interest that provide the political machinery to make sure the leaders remain unassailable at the ballot box.

Dawn Clark Netsch and the Illinois Business Round Table (and the rest of the craven business community) can drag out all the theoretical arguments they want. They are still wrong. Illinois is teeming with hardworking, decent citizens from across the political spectrum.

These citizens would gladly make the sacrifices necessary to enter the political arena. There are plenty of good people that would rise to the occasion and fix Illinois. It is the current constitution, *and the corrupt political class that it created,* that will never let that happen. We see this in our headlines. We know this in our hearts.

Illinois' "leadership problem" cannot be fixed absent a Constitutional Convention because it is the Constitution that created Illinois' patently awful leadership. A new convention, on the other hand, provides the "breakthrough" opportunity for new leadership to emerge without having to sell out to the system first.

They will take our pensions away

This argument is heard most often from the various teacher unions and public section unions. Illinois' constitution includes a pension guarantee that says the pensions are an enforceable contract, which may not be diminished.

Yet, not only has the state **never** adequately funded the pension system, several years the actually took money **from** the pensions to fund pet projects. When people have tried to enforce the pension guarantee the courts have told them no. When legislators are told to lay off the pensions, they threaten to amend the constitution and take the guarantee away.

There are three things currently "protecting" state pensions: contract law, the Illinois Constitution, and federal due process rights. First, the state issues contracts, which do include the pension benefits. Regardless of what a lawmaker says, the state is bound by their contracts.

The Illinois Constitution, Article XII Section 5 states the pension guarantee as previously pointed out. However, the state has not only never lived up to their side of the deal; they have even taken money out.

Lastly, federal courts have ruled that pension benefits are a "property right" that may not be taken without due process. What this means is that if the Illinois Constitution were amended today saying, "All state pensions are confiscated and the money is to be put in the General Fund.", it would take one lawsuit in a federal court to have a federal judge reverse that amendment. Federal due process rights transcend a state constitution.

The best someone could do who wants to wiggle out of the pension system is to simply not offer pensions to new employees and the state can do that today if they so desire.

It should be noted that the only plan to reform the pension system so that it can be fully funded and enforceable is contained in this book. Neither the unions nor the business community nor legislative leaders have offered any plan to ensure the viability of the pension system. The problem is not the generosity of the pensions (though high-ranking administrators have abused the system to their own benefit); it is that the state is under no real obligation to keep its promises. Our plan fixes Illinois pension problems. It does not destroy them. If you are covered by Illinois' pensions, nothing threatens your retirement more than the "status quo."

There is no intellectually sound argument against a Convention

We ask that the citizens of Illinois stop listening to the jaundiced pundits and the intellectually flabby political class. We ask that you trust the people of Illinois.

Is it possible that some bad people get elected as delegates? Yes, but we know that some good people will be elected delegates as well.

Is it possible to fix Illinois with out a Constitution? We challenge you to offer us a plausible scenario. Absent changes, what incentives are there for our political class to begin any kind of reform? We argue that there are none.[8] This is *the* debate in which we need to be engaged.

Now that we've explained how bad things are in Illinois, and how only a convention can fix things, it is time for us to show you just how good our Constitution could be.

---

[8] We welcome your input at www.illinoiscitizenscoalition.com.

Here is an interesting thing to keep in mind. Virtually no one is arguing against the reforms we lay out in the next section. Even the people against the convention support many, if not all, of these reforms. One look at them and you may notice that they are very similar to some that have already been introduced into the General Assembly - but have never been called even for an initial vote. This should show anyone that reform through the General Assembly is impossible, as is the ability to elect any independent Representatives.

Remember this!

Voting "Yes" offers the opportunity for positive change. Voting "No" offers nothing at all (other than rubberstamping the status quo.)

Potential Reforms

The point of a constitutional convention doesn't end with a list of all that is wrong with state government. There are countless letters to the editors, radio talk shows, television shows and blogs with which to vent a list of complaints about how the state is being run.

A constitutional convention should be undertaken to fix those problems with concrete reforms designed to directly address problems.

> **About this Section**
>
> In this portion of the book, we propose specific changes to Illinois Constitution, as well as the reasons for those changes. We believe all these properly shift the balance of power in Illinois in favor of Illinois citizens.
>
> We have also included some "Model Language" that might be written into a new Illinois Constitution. This language will be marked as such.
>
> We also intend to post an entire "Model Constitution" on our website (www.myillinoisconstitution.org) in a format that allows citizens to critique, debate, and propose changes.

It is also important to re-emphasize that *a constitution is a framework for governance*. It is should not become a behemoth of legislation, a codification of special interests, or a mechanism for partisan hacks to settle scores. The European Union Constitution - which failed to be ratified by the citizens of that continent in 2005 - was about 480 pages long or about 40 times larger by word count than the United States Constitution. A state constitution should provide the basics of how a government will work and perform its functions in language that is simple and accessible to its citizens.

That said, what follows are six major concrete reforms that we believe Illinois Constitution should include. There are six tertiary reforms, which we present in less detail. You, as an interested Illinois citizen, may have other ideas. We encourage you to vote "yes" in November, and run for delegate and campaign on your ideas. Illinois needs you.

Recall Elections

In a democratic society, shouldn't the people have the ability to remove a sitting politician who no longer chooses to serve the public interest? Is it really advisable or recommended that a politician be allowed to serve his full term after he or she has exposed himself being unable or unwilling to lead? Does the public really needed to be saddled with an obviously corrupt or inept politician who continues in office simply because his colleagues refuse to impeach him?

Currently, Illinois' governor, Rod Blagojevich, has approval ratings that sink below even the Unites States Congress. He proposed a massive tax increase plan that was voted down unanimously by the Illinois House in 2007 and then refused to discuss anything meaningful for the state budget until well after the deadline for the budget. The General Assembly had to exclude him from budget discussions. A governor who has so alienated the General Assembly where they simply ignore him and move forward without him has lost the ability to lead. The comedy was only magnified by his continual calls for special sessions of the General Assembly which proposed no legislation. The General Assembly started ignoring these proclamations as an egregious abuse of constitutional power.

The question of recalls is not uncontroversial despite its rare use in politics. In the entire history of the American Republic, there have only ever been two governors that have been successfully recalled. Most recent was Gray Davis who was recalled and replaced by Arnold Schwarzenegger in a special election. There are concerns that such elections would be used capriciously to undo a democratically conducted election. History has shown that these concerns are unfounded. Voters have only recalled a sitting statewide politician twice, and in both cases, the politician concerned was exceedingly unpopular. It is important, however, that the threshold for conducting such an action, at the public expense, is not set so low that it can be initiated as a form of electoral harassment.

In order to ensure a high enough level of public support for a recall election, a petition requirement of 10% of the voters of the last election for that office should be established. For instance, to recall Blagojevich one would need a petition that had 348,668 signatures. In 2006, the governor's race had 3,486,671 votes[9]. Recall elections would be available against any elected official at any level of government. A township supervisor who was elected in a race with 4,000 votes would be subject to a recall election with a petition signed by 400 voters eligible to vote in that race.

For statewide offices an additional requirement should be placed on recall petitions to ensure that the support is more-or-less statewide instead of localized, the petition should be required to include signatures equal to 10% of the votes cast for that office in that county in the last election for at least 10 counties. This would ensure, for instance, that Cook County would not be able to stage recall elections at will because they have a substantial proportion of the population of Illinois. Ensuring both a respectable number of signatures and geographic representation will ensure that recall elections will not be forced for capricious reasons. The system outlined above is similar to the system in place in California currently.

Once the recall petitions are received and certified, an election will be scheduled within 90 days on the question of the recall of the public official in question. Upon majority vote, that official will be removed.

This system would allow for unpopular, ineffective, or corrupt politicians to be removed from office sooner than their term would allow. The term "public servants" implies that these officials should be accountable to the people and providing for recall elections would be an avenue to ensure that accountability. It would provide an important check against elected officials to be responsive to their constituents.

As an interesting aside, the question of recall elections has already been discussed and is supported by many politicians in Illinois, including the Governor himself yet most political observers believe the recall amendment that was introduces has no chance of being called for a final vote in the General Assembly so voters will have no ability to ratify such an amendment.

---

[9] Illinois State Board of Elections data, http://www.elections.il.gov/ElectionInformation/VoteTotalsList.aspx?officeid=3780

Model Language – Recalls

(a) Any elected official in the state of Illinois may be subjected to a recall election upon petition from the voters. A petition to recall an elected official must state a reason for the recall.

(b) For statewide officials, a recall petition must be signed by 10% of the number of voters for that official in the last election. Additionally, the petition must contain signatures of 10% of the voters for that office in the election in a given county for 10 different counties in the state.

(c) For officials not elected state-wide, the number of signatures must amount to 10% of the number of voters for that official in the last general election from voters within the jurisdiction of that office.

(d) Any interested voter may submit an affidavit stating they intend to circulate petitions for recall of a particular official and the reason for the recall. Such affidavit shall be filed with the State Board of Elections and the individual has no more than 90 days to circulate petitions and gather the required amount of signatures.

(e) Signatures and petitions may be challenged as provided by law, however, the reason given for recalling an official shall not be subject to adjudication.

(f) No later than 90 days after receiving the required number of signatures, the Secretary of State shall schedule a special election for the recall of the official in question. Where possible and reasonable, the Secretary of State shall schedule such a recall election simultaneously with another scheduled primary or general election.

(g) The question of recalling a particular elected official shall appear in plain language with the given reason stated in the recall petitions. Upon a majority vote, the official shall be immediately removed from office.

(h) The method for replacing a successfully recalled official shall be provided by law.

Term Limits

On cannot enter a discussion on politics without eventually hearing comments "class" in America. Despite that there is no real class in the formal sense of the term (i.e. something you are born into and thus not entitled to change); the term is ubiquitous in politics. Interestingly enough, the one class that rarely gets discussed is the one that really matters, the "political class". These are the people who are in elected or appointed office as a career. Taking a look at almost anyone in office and comparing them to a normal neighbor, one will discover they simply aren't very much like us. The higher the office, the more true this becomes.

There are many reasons for this and reforming the state constitution can only address some. First and foremost, those elected or appointed to public service should do so on a temporary basis. The longer one stays in the government, the less connected they are to the people they represent and less able to clearly articulate and understand their needs. The incumbency advantage is very real and works against to influence of voters on their representatives. If a politician doesn't have to worry about getting thrown out of office, they are less likely to take seriously the legitimate needs and complaints of their constituents.

At the founding of this nation, it was envisioned that legislators would be from the citizenry and serve brief periods and return to their normal jobs. The legislative season is an echo of this historical ideal. Legislators would come to the Capitol for a short time to deal with the needs of the government and then return to their jobs where they were accessible by their constituents and, more importantly, they lived, worked and played in the same environment. The members of Illinois General Assembly, for instance, are only part-time workers. Both the Senate and House are set up so that, in theory, the elected legislators are only in Springfield part-time and the rest of the time is spent in their various professions.

The reality is that term limits are very popular among voters and not very popular among politicians. Voters, rightly distrust politicians who spend their full-time professions for decades in the halls of power. A movement to impose term limits on US Congressmen and Senators was very successful but ultimately failed due to constitutional concerns (such a change on the federal level would require amending the US Constitution). Most states have term limits for their elected officials. There is little downside, even for politicians really, for term limits now that several states have had them for some time.

The particular form of term limits proposed here is that any elected or appointed official will be limited to two terms or eight years, whichever is greater. Further, all terms of office for elected or appointed officials will be limited to a maximum of four years. These term limits will be imposed on every office in the state, from governor down to school board. The only offices that will be exempt are judicial officers who will remain under the retention system that they currently enjoy.

The one point of deviation in this proposal from how term limits are implemented in other states is the imposition of limits on appointed officials. In some ways, it is more important to limit appointment terms that elected officials because those individuals are not elected by the people of the state, nor subject to recall, reelection, or any of the other forms of influence people have over elected officials. Yet these appointed officials enjoy a great deal of authority over state matters and exert a good deal of political power over the citizenry. In some cases, appointments are handed out as political favors, in others "blue ribbon" appointments are made to ensure no real work gets done. By imposing term limits here, the damage made by bad appointments is mitigated.

This won't prevent someone from making a career in politics, per se. However, by limiting the time they can stay in a particular office, it makes it more difficult. A popular an effective leader will likely be able to rise through the ranks, which is an incentive we can all deal with. Unpopular politicians will see there terms expire and have to return to private life. It's not an ideal fix, but it moves us closer to a democratic ideal and will lead to fresh blood being brought into office to deal with problems hopefully in new ways.

Model Language - Term Limits

Members of the General Assembly shall be elected at the general election in even-numbered years. Members of the General Assembly shall be limited to serving a maximum of eight years or two terms of no longer than four years in each of the chambers during their lifetime. (In Legislative Article)

Any elected office established under this article for a unit of local government or a school board shall be subject to term limits. No person may serve for more than 2 terms of a maximum of 4 years. Any person appointed to a governing or oversight body created by a unit of local government shall be limited to serving a maximum of 2 terms of not more than 4 years in length. (In Local Government Article)

No one shall be elected or appointed to serve more than eight years total in any one Executive Branch position under this Article. In applying this section, service in any existing Executive position resulting from an election or appointment prior to the effective date of this section shall not be counted. (In Executive Article)

Open Ballots and Open Primaries

The problem of entrenched politicians is not, however, just a factor of the ability to be in a single elected office for an entire career. The other problem is that in Illinois ballot access for independent or third-party candidates is far more difficult than being a candidate for an "established" party. On top of this obstacle, even for an average citizen to run under an established party is difficult because the primary system forces average voter to disclose their political affiliation. The result is that primary elections have far lower turnout than general elections. Those who do turn out are not representative of society as a whole which ends up that, in many cases, the two choices on the ballot are both unacceptable to the citizenry as a whole.

As an example, the 2006 election for governor of Illinois pitted Rod Blagojevich against Judy Baar-Topinka. In both cases, the general approval rating of both candidates was remarkably poor, even among those who identified with the same party as the candidate. Yet a combination of difficult ballot access and a closed primary that encourages low voter turnout allowed for two candidates who, on their own, would not be the desired choice of voters across the political spectrum.

Democracy, or more accurately a democratic Republic, is predicated on the idea of choice. There can be no real freedom if there are no real choices. Free association is meaningless if there is only one association, for instance. The same is true with the right to vote. If neither candidate is truly acceptable to the citizens, there exists no real choice to choose otherwise. The ballot in 2006 was a choice between thoroughly corrupt candidate A versus thoroughly corrupt candidate B, both of whom has been or are under federal investigation for corruption. A free nation should not have to endure voting under a condition of "picking the worst of two evils."

There is an additional reason to adopt open ballot access. In 2006, a federal lawsuit against the vast disparity in requirements between the established parties compared to third party candidates resulted in the Illinois ballot access system being declared unconstitutional by the 7th Circuit Court of Appeals[10]. The court has since directed the law to be revised to not infringe the "fundamental right to access to the ballot" and such reforms have failed in the General Assembly. The court called Illinois' rules the strictest in the nation and has been used by the major parties to keep independent candidates off the ballot. The only change the General Assembly has made to date is reducing the signature requirement for independent or new candidates from 10% to 5%. For comparison, established parties only need .5%.

To run for United States Senator for Illinois in 2008, a Republican, Democratic, or Green Party (which recently became "established") candidate would have to gather 5,000-10,000 signatures. A new party or independent candidate has to gather at least 25,000 signatures. That is five times the minimum for an established party. To run for US Congress in the 15th district, about 800 signatures is required for an established party (only 600 for Greens), but an independent or new party candidate needs at least 10,217 signatures. That's about twelve times more than an established party.

This system is obviously designed to keep "outsiders" off the ballot and stacks the cards against establishing a new party for the purposes of the law. The General Assembly has not demonstrated the leadership to fix a system they've been required to fix, it should fall to the Constitutional Convention to fix it for them.

As far as ballot access is concerned, there should be no discrimination based on political affiliation whatsoever in the requirements for running for office. Additionally, the requirements of being listed on the ballot should remain low enough to not be onerous to individual candidates yet still demonstrate a basic level of support among the voters. In short, for candidates of third parties or for independents, the requirements for running for office should be identical to those requirements for established-party candidates (i.e. Democrats and Republicans). The petition requirements for running as a candidate should be no more than

---

[10] Lee v Keith, et al, 7th Circuit of Appeals, #05-4355

1% of the voters for that office in the last elections, but can be less as established by the General Assembly.

The second reform, open primaries, is extremely popular but very controversial. The argument against them, one that is accepted by the Supreme Court of the United States, is that free association requires the ability to define who is not a member of a group. This means that the parties have a right to establish who can and cannot vote for who will be the "standard bearer" for the party in the race for a political office. All open primary systems to date have been declared unconstitutional by the courts. The last open primary system, Louisiana's, has been abandoned for a more "traditional" primary system. Yet such a reform is still popular to the voters.

The problem with this argument is that most voters do not formally associate with a political party. That system that made sense 50 years ago simply does not exist as such today. Most voters don't donate to the party, have not filled out formal registrations to a political party, or attend any party functions. In voting in a primary system, such a voter needs to publicly disclose their political affiliation, which can lead to personal problems. For instance, many in academia simply do not vote in primaries to avoid the harassment of their colleagues. Many clergy, who believe in public participation but do not want to affiliate their religion for use in partisan talking points will not vote in primaries to avoid such a conflict. The result is that most voters are alienated by the closed party system, turnout is remarkably low, and voters end up being presented by less-than-acceptable candidates. However, the legal obstacles are real and need to be addressed.

Most voters are Republicans or Democrats simply for the purposes in voting for a primary. Taking a ballot for that party in a primary is what substitutes for "party registration" in Illinois. It is important to note, the not even the parties really take this party affiliation seriously. In almost every primary election in recent memory, a primary candidate (usually several) advocate for voters in other parties to take a ballot in their party's primary to vote for them. It seems the parties' concern about party registration only is brought up when the question of an open primary is concerned.

To overcome this, party registration will be required to be formal. Namely, a voter who wants to be a registered Republican will have to file such a registration with the election officials of his jurisdiction (subject to whatever requirements a party wishes to impose) by the voter registration deadline for the election they wish to vote in. This registration will be public and available to those who wish to examine such a record.

To create a system that maximizes ballot access and voter participation, the primary system should be abolished as such. There will be only a general election where anyone who meets the set criteria applicable to everyone to get on the ballot will be listed on the ballot. The parties, at their sole discretion and expense, will determine which candidates are members of their party for the purposes of putting the party designation on the ballot. If they wish, they can have multiple candidates with the party designation or only one candidate. No candidate will be able to be in multiple parties, however. It the parties wish to fund their own primaries that is fine, but it will only affect which candidate gets to have (R) or (D) after their name. Any candidate that does not drop out and does not get the party to allow them to use the party designation will be listed as an independent for the election.

This will potentially lead to a crowded field of candidates on a ballot where no one gets 50% and the winner may get substantially less than that. To overcome this problem, for any race that does not have a winner of the majority vote the top two vote getters will compete in a run-off election 21 days later which will determine the winner.

The only exception to this reform will be the race for United States President and party delegates to the convention as that particular race is so governed by federal law; such a reform would be unworkable and only lead to side-lining Illinois for the sake of picking presidential candidates.

Open ballots and open primaries will allow for greater participation not only among voters, but among those who would run for office. Many people have commented that the low level of public participation in elections is a dangerous attribute of a democracy. Elected officials should have to earn the support of the greatest number of citizens possible to ensure the responsiveness and integrity of our Republic.

Model Language – Open Primaries

(a) This section shall apply to all elections except the primary election for President of the United States and the delegates to the national party committees for the selection of a presidential candidate.

(b) Any candidate who meets the criteria for being listed as a candidate for election for office in a general election shall be listed on the ballot for the general election. A candidate may elect to drop out of an election no later than 30 days prior to the date of the general election.

(c) Political parties, at their own expense, may conduct primaries or caucuses to determine which candidate is the designated candidate for the party in an election for elected office. Parties may restrict such designation to only one candidate but are not required to do so.

(d) No later than 60 days prior to an election, the political party will certify to the election officials responsible for the election in question which candidate or candidates are designated to represent the party in the general election. Those candidates will have a designation after their name on the ballot indicating their political affiliation.

(e) No candidate may be a designated candidate of multiple political parties.

(f) Any candidate not designated by a political party as that parties' candidate shall be listed as an independent on the general election ballot.

(g) In the case of more than 2 candidates running for the same office, any candidate receiving a majority vote shall be certified the winner of the election. If no candidate receives a majority vote, the top 2 vote recipients shall compete in a run-off election 21 days after the general election. The highest vote recipient in the run-off election shall be certified the winner in the run-off election. In the case of only one or two candidates running for the same office, the highest vote recipient shall be certified the winner of the election.

(h) In races where more than one seat for the same office is open (i.e. multi-member districts, school boards, etc), the highest vote recipients shall be certified as the winners of the elections. There shall be no run-off elections in these races.

(i) "Slating" of candidates by political parties is prohibited.

Model Language – Ballot Access

All elections shall be free and equal, and accessible for any political party or candidate that meets requirements set forth in this Constitution and by the General Assembly.

Any laws or regulations that operate to favor one party or parties, by definition, deprive citizens that are not members of those parties of the equal protection of the laws. Any law or regulation that favors or hinders an individual to run for elected office based on political affiliation or non-affiliation is prohibited.

Binding Citizen Referenda

What happens when necessary reforms are popular among the citizens, important for continued viability of the state, yet elected leaders lack the courage or conviction to make such a change? Or worse, what happens when the elected leaders adopt a legal regime that is directly against the interests of the citizens of the state at large but fall short of a constitutional question? The case of ballot access above is a great example of this; despite being required to by the outcome of a federal lawsuit the legislature has not taken the appropriate action. Right now, the citizens possess little to no check on legislative power in this case.

Currently, citizens do have a method to place a referendum on the ballot for an election but such a referendum is advisory only and subject to legal maneuvers to even knock those referenda off the ballot for capricious reasons. A democratic republic should have some method for citizens to act in those cases where the elected leaders either: (a) are acting directly against the public will, (b) refuse to act in cases where action is clearly necessary. However, it is important to prevent frivolous referendum on the ballot that have no real public support but yet take up costs to election officials. Some level of public support that is reasonable but doesn't present an insurmountable obstacle should be required in terms signatures for a ballot petition.

A petition to list a referendum on the ballot in a general election should require signatures in the amount of 5% of the votes in the last general election for the governor. Additionally, 5% of five counties must be achieved as well to ensure a sufficient geographic level of support. Such a referendum will be binding law in the state subject to over-ruling or over-turning by being declared unconstitutional (state or federal), a later referendum, or a constitutional amendment. A referendum will pass and become binding based on a simple majority of those who vote on the question within 90 days of the vote being certified.

Additionally, citizens will have the ability to list a constitutional amendment for vote on the ballot without approval from the General Assembly. Such an amendment must be supported by a petition signed by 10% of the number of votes in the last general election race for governor and 10% in at least five counties. Additionally, such an amendment will pass based on a vote of at least two-thirds of the voters who vote on such an amendment. Before an amendment becomes law, it must pass twice in two consecutive general elections with two-thirds (i.e. in 2008 and 2010, or 2010 and 2012, etc).

Having a two-vote requirement separated by two years will allow a "cooling off" period to ensure such amendments are sufficiently thought through before they become codified. The General Assembly will still retain the right to amend the constitution but will have to bring such amendments up for a vote in a general election and be supported by two-thirds. However, in amendments initiated by the General Assembly, only one general election vote will be necessary.

Such reforms will additionally increase public participation and enable voters to influence their elected officials. Even referenda that fail still can have influence and lead to ultimate compromise legislative action. Many will object with concerns of a "tyranny of the majority" objection. Such an objection is unfounded. In cases of binding referendum, questions will still be subject to constitutional scrutiny on the state and federal level. The latitude for true oppressive referendum is extremely small.

However, more importantly it leads to a question, who is more trustworthy and less likely to oppress, government officials with power and money who tend to be less-than-responsive to voters, or the average citizen living in a community who have to deal with the effects of such action directly? If we cannot trust a majority of voters not to run completely out-of-line it isn't a question of whether referendum a good idea, it is a question of whether a democratic republic is a good idea. It is telling, however, that usually the people who are loudest in objecting to a "tyranny of the majority" seem quite content to allow a "tyranny of the minority" which has been historically far more destructive to human rights.

Amending the constitution should be a difficult task whether it is undertaken by the General Assembly or by the citizens themselves. Such an amendment comes with a significant amount of power as the "supreme law of the state" and it should be widely supported by a larger number of citizens than a simple law should have. It is important to emphasize, that either amendments or referendum are still subject to the United States Constitution which does highly protect rights of minorities.

Legislative Reforms

The General Assembly is no small source of the problems plaguing the state. The pension crisis, for instance, is largely one of the creations of the legislature. Chronic over-spending, hidden member initiatives, and legislative tricks to hide legislation from the public all contribute to an out-of-control body that drives taxes up not because of necessity in providing services, but to bail out the immense waste, graft, and pork in the budget.

Most of the major legislative decisions are made by the "four tops", the party leaders of each chamber. During the budget crisis in 2007 when the state went almost two months into the fiscal year without having the authority to pay its bills, most of the legislators stopped showing up to sessions because they simply had nothing to do. The four tops did the negotiating and the rank-and-file were simply waiting for the decision to come down. What is the point of having a legislative system of 59 Senators and 118 Representatives when only 4 make the important calls?

There are a bundle of reforms that address the wide problems facing the legislature. The first is the abolition of shell bills. Shell bills are pieces of legislation that are basically empty and go through the entire legislative process until the end when they are amended with their true content. This allows legislators to hide their policies and legislation until the last minute when the put it on their colleagues desk and insist they vote on it. The abusiveness of this practice hardly needs much explanation. All legislation that is passed will be required by the new constitution to be substantially similar to the language it had when it was introduced. Bills passed by one house and sent to another must be sent back in substantially similar terms. The House can pass an appropriations bill on schools and the Senate amends it and passes a bill that legalizes a Chicago land-based casino. The public has a right to see legislation and contribute to it as it goes through the process.

As a necessary corollary to the above, all legislation before it receives its final vote should be available for public inspection and comment for 7 days. What this means is before one chamber passes and send legislation to another, it must be publicly available for 7 days. Additionally, when differing versions of the same bill are passed in both houses, the final compromise bill must be available for 7 days before the final vote to send the bill to the Governor.

The ability of a leader of a chamber to kill bills, even though they may pass easily if called for a vote is unacceptable. The rules committee could be renamed to "the place where good bills go to die" and it would more accurately reflect its role. To check this abusive practice, any bill that is joined on the motion of at least one-third of a chamber, must be called for a floor vote.

Lastly, all appropriations must be itemized by recipient. In 2007, the Senate passed a $200+ million dollar package of "member initiatives" which were not visible to the public because they were packaged together. It may be difficult to get rid of pork all-together, but all of these so-called "member initiatives" should be disclosed to the public so that truly wasteful spending can be appropriately dealt with.

There reforms will shed some sunlight into the General Assembly and the legislative process. The people have a fundamental right to contribute to the legislative process and these reforms will open that process up and allow for sincere and informed contribution. It will also check the power of the chamber leaders to enforce a political agenda that is not well-supported in the chamber and ideally, with the public at large.

Pension Reform

The State of Illinois, according to some estimates, is approximately $100 billion in debt because of chronic under-funding of the pension system. Despite the current constitution requiring a balanced budget, accounting games have allowed the state to shirk the obligations it made to state employees in funding the pension system. As of this writing, the state is now delaying most payments out of the general fund because it cannot pay bills on time. If Illinois were a private entity, it would be legally bankrupt at this point. While pensions seem to be a single-issue question, the enormous state debt (approximately 2 times the entire state budget for a year) presents a dramatic economic crisis that is in immediate need of resolution.

The current pension system in the way it has been designed has contributed to this massive pension problem. Additionally, subjected pension contributions to annual budget appropriations in the General Assembly infuse pension obligations into the political system where games are likely to be played. Despite guaranteeing pensions in the constitution, in 2005 the General Assembly actually dipped into the pension fund to appropriate money for pork-barrel projects. The General Assembly has shown themselves to be poor stewards of such a system that not only affects state employees and their pensions, but has brought dire economic consequences to that state and its citizens as a whole.

To address the economic concern, currently the state has to appropriate pension contributions to the various pension funds directly. The various agencies and school systems do not contribute the "employer contribution", the state does. This has led to an incentive problem, which was most recently seen in the Teacher Retirement System.

As budgets tightened, school officials looked for ways to save money. Since payroll is the biggest or one of the biggest components of a school budget, that was a logical place to start. They offered teachers who were close to retirement significant raises to encourage them to retire early on an artificially increased pension. Teachers liked the idea because their pension would be higher than it would be otherwise and they could retire early to boot. Administrators like the idea because they could replace experienced and higher-paid teachers with lower-paid less-experienced teachers and lighten the load on their budget.

Since the state, and not the employing school, pays the "employer's contribution" the state ended up subsidizing the difference. The result was a compromised pension system that was weighed down by pushing pensions higher than the system could tolerate. It wasn't, however, a school administrator's problem because pensions weren't in their budget nor were the required to address the problem. In essence, they solved one of their problems by making another (and bigger) problem for another agency.

The solution can be found in looking at another retirement system and how it maintains integrity for its members. The Illinois Municipal Retirement Fund provides pensions for over 2,000 local units of government and relies on no state appropriations. It does this through contributions out of a member's paycheck, contributions from the employing agency directly, and from investment earnings of the fund as a whole. Risk is segmented by employer by forcing employers to come up with money to compensate for "creative pension schemes." Basically, if the City of Wheaton tries to game the pension of some top city staff, it will not risk the pensions for the City of Rantoul.

The reform should take the employer contribution of the pension system out of the hands of the General Assembly which is not reasonably connected to the employees of the pension they are funding (or more accurately not funded). Additionally, by the state subsidizing the pension contributions, it takes the incentive to act appropriately out of the hands of those who are responsible for making budget decisions for the government agency which employees that individual involved.

The agency that employs the individual should be responsible for the pension contributions of their employees. Using the Illinois Municipal Retirement Fund model, pension games will be paid for by the agencies involved that will have to make budget decisions regarding how much money they want to take away from their mission to line pockets of its high-ranking staff.

The transition will not be without difficulty. It will require a one-time "bump" to budgets of agencies throughout the state that will have to absorb this new cost, but can be paid for by diffusing what would have been the full state contribution proportionally among the various state agencies. A proposal to pay down the remaining debt to the pension fund will have to be negotiated in the state legislature. This reform will create a sustainable pension system in which accountability for pension decisions will rest on those who make those decisions.

Additional Reforms

While the above six reforms represent the major issues that would be tackled in a constitutional convention, there are many additional reforms that we suggest be implemented as well to ensure good, open and accountable government. We thought they were important enough to warrant mention in this book.

Property Tax Reform

Should Illinois citizens get the opportunity for a constitutional convention, property tax reform will figure largely. Many citizens are experiencing skyrocketing property tax bills that are forcing homeowners out of their homes. A convention will allow citizens to reform and simplify the Byzantine nature of their property tax system.

Property taxes in Illinois have always been unnecessarily complex. This has resulted in a situation where connected and experienced attorneys have been able to earn a good living challenging property tax assessments on a property-by-property basis. The most effective way to fix this system is too reform and simplify Illinois property tax collection system.

Reform of property classifications, Tax Increment Finance District transparency, and the possible elimination of the *Township* as a governmental entity, and property owner protections should be on the table. Absent a convention, these issues will not get a hearing.

Ending Gerrymandering

Some of those reading this have never have heard of the old cliché regarding gerrymandering. We are supposed to live in a nation where the voters choose their representatives, but gerrymandering allows representatives to choose their voters. As with most of the political issues discussed in this book, (corruption, patronage, nepotism, etc.) a little gerrymandering may seem innocuous, in Illinois however, with one-party rule making it virtually impossible to produce fair district boundaries, the new constitution must return Illinois to a state where the voters choose their representatives, and not vice versa. One need only look at the 4th Congressional District of Illinois to see the problem.

We believe that we should model our constitution clauses regarding writing district boundaries after the state of Iowa.

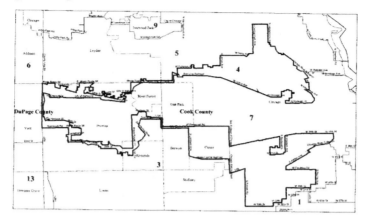

Figure 1. Congressional District 4 Map, From Illinois State Board of Elections

[11]Under Chapter 42 of the Iowa Code, enacted in 1980, the Iowa legislature has the final responsibility for enacting both congressional and state legislative district plans. However, the nonpartisan Legislative Services Bureau starts the process. The Bureau must develop up to three plans that can be accepted or rejected by the legislature. The four criteria for the Bureau's plans, in descending order of importance, are:

1. Population equality
2. Contiguity
3. Unity of counties and cities (maintaining county lines)
4. Compactness.

Chapter 42 specifically forbids the use of political affiliation, previous election results, the addresses of incumbents, or any demographic information other than population in creating the redistricting proposals.[12]

The ideal Constitution would include language modeled after Iowa's Chapter 42.

---

[11] http://en.wikipedia.org/wiki/Image:IL04_109.gif

[12] http://www.centrists.org/pages/2004/07/7_buck_trust.html?0.194884532903419#works

Spending Caps on Every Illinois Governmental Entity

Experience demonstrates that no matter which party is in power, government spending always seems to ratchet upward. This process is held in check only by split government and a robust taxpayers lobby – neither of which exists in Illinois. Illinois no longer has split government, and the taxpayers lobby has become too weak to prevent spending increases. This is why we need spending caps for every governmental entity in the state of Illinois.

Illinois has had some experience with "caps" on taxes. It hasn't been very good. In 1994, a brief period of Republican control of both chambers, Illinois was able to pass "property tax caps" for the "collar counties" of the Chicago metropolitan area. While these caps probably resulted in a slower rate of growth for local governments, the combination of poorly drafted legislation and clever accounting tricks allowed some municipal governments - school districts in particular - too develop work-arounds that gamed the "tax caps."

The property tax simplification, combined with permanent caps that limit the *spending*, (not tax rates) would provide Illinois citizens much need protections from runaway government. The growth of every governmental entity -- from the smallest mosquito abatement district to the Illinois General Revenue Fund – should be limited to **no greater than the rate of inflation plus population growth**.

This spending cap should **not** exempt "new property" or any other streams of government revenue. One reason that taxes and revenue growth has exploded in recent years, is that "tax caps" are applied only to existing property. When a developer built a new subdivision, the taxes for that property created a flood of new revenue. While the tax on existing property was theoretically "capped," the ability to actually lower property taxes by the addition of new revenue was prevented because the new property was exempted from "caps."

On one hand this seems reasonable, given that new construction is entering the revenue stream. On the other hand, by capping *taxes* instead of spending, government was allowed to grow unchecked through the operation of an explosive real estate market. Now that the real estate driven spending binge has ended,

Illinois property owners (residential and business) find themselves with massive growing pension liabilities caused by promises that only could have been kept if real estate kept expanding rapidly…forever. This is why we need hard *spending* caps, not soft *tax* caps.

The new Constitution also needs to address the situation where the government (state or local) wants to expand spending beyond any cap. We believe that if citizens want to expand taxation and spending for new or expanding government services, then a process for such expansion should be available. The difficulty lies in distinguishing between the true will of the citizenry, and the will of a political class that is nearly always more attentive to the special interests that drive government spending.

The new Constitution should solve this problem by allowing the citizens to vote on any new spending and/or taxation beyond the spending cap. This vote should be placed on the ballot automatically - triggered when any governmental body passes laws that will break the cap. Given the attention that such governing bodies pay to spending interests, the citizens deserve the protection of a $3/5^{th}$ super-majority for any vote to break a spending cap.

We therefore recommend that the spending caps, and the process by which they can be raised, be clearly defined in the new constitution. There should be no clause and/or language anywhere in the new constitution that should allow for any ambiguity regarding the governmental entity, its budget, and the specific budget number to which the spending cap applies. This is necessary because of the many current ambiguities and loopholes written into much of Illinois' legislation. The ironically named "tax caps" in suburban counties discussed above are a perfect example.

Model Language – Spending Caps (abridged)

Article VII - SECTION 10 – TAXPAYER BILL OF RIGHTS

(a) General provisions. The preferred interpretation of this section shall reasonably restrain most the growth of government. All provisions are self-executing and severable and supersede conflicting state constitutional, state statutory, charter, or other state or local provisions. Other limits on district revenue, spending, and debt may be weakened only by future voter approval.

(b) Term definitions. Within this section:
(1) "Initiative" means a non-recall petition or referred measure in an election.
(2) "Entity" means the state or any unit of local government.
(3) "Emergency" excludes economic conditions, revenue shortfalls, or district salary or fringe benefit increases.
(4) "Fiscal year spending" means all entity expenditures and reserve increases except, as to both, those for refunds made in the current or next fiscal year or those from gifts, federal funds, collections for another government, pension contributions by employees and pension fund earnings, reserve transfers or expenditures, damage awards, or property sales.
(5) "Inflation" means the percentage change in the United States Bureau of Labor Statistics Consumer Price Index.

(c) **All governmental taxing entities in the state of Illinois shall limit the growth of their budget appropriations and expenditures to no greater than the prior year except for the rate of inflation plus population growth with in the boundaries of that entity.** Should the operation of economic activity reduce an entity's revenue, the highest level of expenditure shall be the foundation from which the entity can calculate its allowable increase.

(d) Excess revenues over allowable expenditures at the end of a fiscal year shall be transferred to a Reserve Fund. The Reserve Fund shall not exceed 3% of the current year's expenditures. Expenditures from the Reserve Fund may be made only upon the exhaustion of other available funds.

Improved Eminent Domain Protections

The recent KELO decision by the US Supreme Court allowed for the taking of private property for private use -- a result that would have most of our founding fathers spinning in their graves. To be sure, the majority of the court could never admit that they were allowing a "taking" for private use. They hid behind the fig leaf of "tax revenues" and say "public purpose." While it is certainly worth while to debate issues of what constitutes "blight," and whether a municipality or state may benefit from converting land to its "highest and best use," your average Illinois Citizen knows a bad deal when he sees one.

Here in Illinois, there are many attempts by cities to use a loose definition of the word "blighted" to condemn properties to turn over to developers and national retail chains.

In a government-driven *taking* in Arlington Heights, a perfectly good mall was called "blighted" to make way for a Target. The owner of the mall reportedly even had the city interfere with tenant contracts, as a city official allegedly told a tenant seeking a permit "not to bother" because the mall was going to be condemned.

In a Lincoln Park neighborhood of Chicago, a series of properties and businesses where threatened with an eminent domain taking. To make matters worse, the city was using its power to benefit developers inside an opaque TIF (Tax Increment Financing) District.

The Chicago Reader, a local free newspaper serving neighborhoods across the city, wrote;

> "On top of all that, the use of TIFs makes a mockery of the rights of property owners, as the merchants on Western Avenue are learning. Traditionally the city reserves its power of eminent domain for large-scale projects—parks, schools, hospitals, highways—that benefit the public. With TIFs in the picture, the city effectively uses eminent domain to transfer property from one private owner to another—typically to a well-connected developer."[13]

---

[13]Chicago Reader On-line -
http://www.chicagoreader.com/features/stories/theworks/070914/

The abuses listed above are only two instances. As we've discussed these issues with citizens across Illinois, we've found that government abuse of eminent domain powers is an increasing concern. There is a massive potential for abuse under the Kelo decision. That, combined with the lack of transparency in Illinois Government, causes us to advocate for stronger protection against eminent domain abuses.

Therefore, a new Illinois constitution should contain clauses that clearly define the differences between "public use" and private interests, strictly prohibiting the use of eminent domain "takings" for the latter. The language in these clauses should clearly limit takings for "blight," as well as place the burden of proof on the government entity to prove its case. This affords the private citizen the maximum protection possible in any dispute.

Model Language – Right of Eminent Domain

Art. I – SECTION 17

(a) Private property shall not be taken or damaged for public use without just compensation as provided by law. Such compensation shall be determined by a jury as provided by law.

(b) For the purposes of this section, the burden of proof shall be on the government agency initiating an eminent domain action.

(c) For the purposes of this section, Property owners shall be entitled to a jury trial to determine a finding that a property constitutes "blight," or any other similar description.

(d) Definitions pertaining to this section;

> (1)"Public use" shall be defined as resulting in public ownership for an express public purpose. Enhancement of revenues for government agencies shall be insufficient as a "public use."
> (2)"Damaged" shall include any substantial diminution of value through regulation by a government agency.

(e) Only real property may be taken via eminent domain action and any property so taken must be held by the governing body for a period of no less than 50 years before which it cannot be transferred, sold or leased to any private body.

(f) Just compensation shall be computed by a jury on the real property by determining the fair market value of the property before eminent domain action was contemplated and adding 10% to cover relocation costs. If the eminent domain action takes over 12 months to complete, a jury shall also add in inflation and a reasonable estimate of appreciation of the market value for the time it takes to complete such action.

Open and Transparent Government

On paper, the Illinois constitution appears to create all the necessary processes for "open government." In operation however, the combination of a poorly written and interpreted Illinois constitution and a political class that works feverishly to keep its activities out of the view of the citizenry, has given Illinois one of the most opaque governments of the 50 states.

Transparent and open government, more than any other issue, transcends the left/right, Democrat/Republican divide. Well intentioned political activists in both parties and from across the political spectrum have become frustrated with the wholesale purchase of their respective parties by powerful and entrenched interests.

Rather than attempt to provide a list of examples, we suggest you read the headlines of your local Illinois paper. One can find examples of waste, fraud, corruption, pork, and patronage in the headlines of nearly every major and minor paper or newscast in Illinois. The time has come for Illinois citizens to rise up and create a "good government" constitution that circumvents the existing Illinois political class.

To that end, the new Illinois Constitution should contain the following clauses that apply to every Illinois governmental unit, including *Home Rule* communities (should *Home Rule* be retained).

- Names of all elected officials, administrative officials, their responsibilities, and contact information, including email addresses
- The name of the FOIA (Freedom of Information Act) compliance person for the agency, and how to contact that person, as well as complete information about how to file a public records request with the agency
- Budget Data (historical budgets and current budget), and a graph showing increases or decreases over time. This should include a uniform "Sources and Uses" statement.
- All Meeting minutes and meeting agendas for the past year
- Information about any lobbying/political advocacy organization the agency supports with its dues—the name of

those organizations, the amount of dues paid to each, and the legislative agenda that each lobbying organization is supporting/opposing.[14]
- A uniform, clear description of the agency's approach to all vendor contracts, how it requests proposals and bids, and copies of all vendor contracts over a certain dollar amount.
- Copies of audits and compliance reports.
- Agency Ethics Codes or Ethics Ordinances
- All agencies' checkbook registers must be placed on-line in a uniform manner.

Most importantly, the new Illinois Constitution should create a legal "cause of action" for any citizen or organization that can present a prima fascia case that a government agency has failed to comply with the above mandates. This cause of action should include sanctions (fines and/or censure) of the public official(s) who obstruct the public's access to information. We believe this innovation is very important.

Like the phantom "balanced budget clause" in our current Constitution, the clauses discussing the *Freedom of Information* are virtually unenforceable for the average citizen. A recent series of articles in the Springfield Journal-Register on the Illinois Freedom of Information Act started off with the following paragraph;

> The Illinois Freedom of Information Act made Illinois the last state to enact legislation that guarantees your right of access to many types of information. An act that was designed to facilitate citizen involvement in government, however, has in practice largely become an exercise in frustration.

In effect, the changes we advocate above are intended to place a great deal of governmental data **in front** of any *Freedom of*

---

[14] The authors believe it may just be a better policy to prohibit government officials (elected and administrative) from using ANY public funds to pay for memberships to such associations. Few people understand that most school boards automatically pay for each member to join the IASB (Illinois Association of School Boards). Taxpayer funds should not be expended for this purpose.

Information Act wall, while simultaneously putting government officials on notice that all information regarding their actions belongs to the public that they putatively serve.

Model Language – Budget Transparency

Article VII – SECTION I – GENERAL PROVISIONS

(a) Public funds, property or credit shall be used only for public purposes.

(b) The State, units of local government and school districts shall incur obligations for payment or make payments from public funds only as authorized by law or ordinance.

(c) Reports and records of the obligation, receipt and use of public funds of the State, units of local government and school districts are public records. **Every Governmental Entity in the State of Illinois shall make available to the public for inspection, any and all reports, accounts, account balances, records of disbursements, and any other communication relating the entity's financial position. This availability for inspection shall be completed within 48 hours, without citizen request, any transaction involving public funds. This disclosure of information shall be posted electronically, in a uniform fashion.**

Home Rule Reform

Article 7, Section 6 of the current Constitution lays out the powers of "Home Rule" units of local government. The standard definition of Home Rule, which is what you are given when your local trustees and city managers ask you to support "Home Rule" in your community, is that it empowers "local government" over the state government. The fact is that it really doesn't do that at all.

True, the current structure of Illinois Home Rule basically empowers the local government, but not against the state. What "Home Rule" in Illinois really does is shield the politicians from citizen initiative, referendum, and oversight. By now this shouldn't be a surprise. The Illinois Constitution was written to empower government, not citizens.

Specifically, the flaw in the Illinois version of home rule is that it denies citizens the right to control local government with a *city charter or constitution.* Other states allow or even mandate that citizens establish a local charter or constitution to control local government before home rule powers are granted. Citizens of Illinois deserve to have the same rights as the citizens of other states.[15]

Model Language – Home Rule

The special privileges of **Home Rule** enjoyed by various local units of government are nullified as of the next general election after this Constitution's ratification. Any governmental unit may become "home rule" by referenda of the people affected initiated either by the governmental body or the people in question. Such a referendum must include a constitution or charter which established which of the "home rule" powers the body does or does not have and how they may be used. A later referenda initiated by the people or the governmental body itself may add, remove, change any or all of the "home rule" powers a government body has. The requirements for a citizen-initiated referendum on home rule powers shall be the same as those specified in Section 13 of this Article.

---

[15] www.illinoisconcon.com, by John Gile

Illinois merely allows the local trustees of cities and villages to dictate policy absent any document or ground rules that protect citizens from abuse. Of course, on paper, it appears that you can change your trustees in the next election. Unfortunately, as we mentioned before, the natural operation of politics dictate that interests benefiting from taxes and regulation have massive advantages over the average citizen.

First, spending interests get large contracts while you get a small tax increase (thousands of small tax increases do add up, however). Second, because their financial (or regulatory) interests are greater than yours, they will always know more than you do about the specific topic at hand.

Result of Reforms

The end result of all of these reforms is to empower citizens. We believe the reforms will produce a strong framework for good government that is makes our government accessible and accountable to the citizenry. Though we have not yet done polling on these reforms, we would be willing to bet that all of these changes enjoy significant public support.

Conclusion

What we have laid forth, we believe, is a solid platform of change in the way that Illinois governs. It will reduce the power of entrenched interests and make it possible for honest voters to fully participate in the political system and make it possible for those good candidates who have been shut out of politics in the past to have a chance to compete for office.

There are many problems that this state faces that are unaddressed, by design, in this constitution. Health care reform is high on the list of voter priorities, but such specific and highly variable issues should be left to the legislative process. A constitution also cannot prevent corrupt individuals from getting elected. What this constitution does do is make it easier to find these individuals, easier to prosecute them for their crimes and easier to remove them from office when they no longer serve the public interest.

Many of these problems can only be corrected by changing the constitution of the state. We have seen that the General Assembly has become unable to address some of these fundamental structural problems such as the balanced budget requirement, ending gerrymandering or enacting term limits. Many of these problems can *only* be corrected in a constitution. A convention represents our only chance to get these sorely needed reforms into place.

The task at hand now is for honest voters to spread the word about this important question that will be on the ballot November 4th, 2008. We believe that Illinois deserves better and all honest citizens must act on this belief before we start to get a government that responds to the public. It is time to stop surrendering to fear and to act boldly while we still have that opportunity to fix the dire problems that face the state.

Write letters to the editor, talk with family and friends and call in to talk radio to discuss the issue. Attend civic or other public meetings and advocate for a convention and these reforms. Consider running as a delegate yourself or finding someone you respect and asking them to do so. Getting a convention will take work. Also, electing reform-minded delegates will not be easy. Together, however, we can make a difference. To that end, the authors have initiated a Speaker's Bureau of advocates for a convention. These speakers come from all points of the political compass, and can effectively lay out why a convention is a great idea.

We need you to be the eyes and ears of the citizenry. If you see that there will a Constitutional Convention Forum or debate, get involved. Contact us, and we will help persuade citizens that the benefits of a convention far, far outweigh any risks.

Learn more about the constitutional convention and the reform agenda or to get involved please go to our website at http://www.illinoiscitizenscoalition.com. A convention is only possible if interested citizens work together to get involved and make our voices heard. Additionally, you can contact the authors by email at jcb@illinoiscitizenscoalition.com or bruno@illinoiscitizenscoalition.com.

Lastly, a draft constitution is available at http://www.myillinoisconstitution.org. This site has forums and provides the ability to comment and revise each section of our draft. Additionally, we use the latest wiki technology to allow any interested citizen to write his or her own component (or entire) constitution. We strive to hear from as many interested Illinois citizens as possible to draw up a constitution worthy of the great citizens of this state.

About the Authors

John C. A. Bambenek is an academic professional at the University of Illinois Urbana-Champaign and co-founder of the Illinois Citizens Coalition. Additionally, he is executive director of the Tumaini Foundation which supports AIDS orphans and other disadvantaged children in Tanzania to get an education. He is considered one of the nation's top experts in information security and is a columnist on political and cultural issues. He is a life-long Illinois resident currently residing in Champaign, Illinois.

Bruno Behrend is currently the host of a Radio Show on WKRS - 1220 AM broadcasting out of Waukegan, Illinois. He is also a consultant to the non-profit sector and a licensed Illinois Lawyer.

He has a background in various areas, including:

- Public Policy Research
- Database Consulting
- Real Estate Investing and Renovation
- Corporate Seminar and Training Development

Mr. Behrend is a graduate of University of Illinois (1983) with a degree in Finance, and a graduate of IIT-Kent College of Law (1990). He is a life-long Illinois resident currently residing in River Forest, Illinois.